The Smart Fir Seller's Guide

How to Make The Most Money When Selling
Your Home

Thomas.K.Lutz

OUTLINE OF THE FIRST-TIME HOME SELLER'S GUIDE

CHAPTER 1: MAKING THE DECISION TO SELL – IMPORTANT CONSIDERATIONS

Alternatives To Selling

Space: Extend House, Rent Rooms

Relocation: Rent Home, "Buy to let" Mortgage, Rent Under Existing Mortgage

Finances: Extend Mortgage, Remortgage

Lifetime Mortgage

Home Reversion Loan

House-Swapping or Part-Exchange

Selling – Where To Begin

Timing: When To Sell, National and Local Housing Market, Interest Rates, Lenders

Buying And Selling: Both At The Same Time, Selling First, Buying First

Budget For Your Sale: Energy Performance Certificate (EPC), Estate Agent's Fee, Solicitors' Fees, Lender's Fees, Removal Costs, Rental Costs, Tax, Other Circumstantial Costs

Considering Assistance

CHAPTER 2: CONSIDERING ASSISTANCE AS A FIRST TIME HOME SELLER

Selecting A Top Realtor – Considerations

FSBO (For Sale By Owner)

Internet: Competition, Short Sales, Foreclosures

Top Producers VS Other Agents

Interview Questions

Contract Types: Open Listing, Agency Listing, Right-To-Sell Listing

The Right Hire - What To Expect

Quality Traits: Honesty, Skill, Professionalism, Creativity, Proven
    Results, Personal Reputation
Quality Techniques: Connections, Technology, Marketing Plan
Complaints Process Protection

CHAPTER 3: PREPARING THE HOME FOR SALE – FIRST IMPRESSIONS

A Good First Impression

Maintenance And Repairs
The Art of "Staging"
Personal Touches
Low-Cost Projects: Painting, Lighting, Simple Yet Modern
Home Inspections

De-Cluttering Tips

The Illusion Of Space
Secret Technique: Opposite Mirrors
Possessions: Storage, Auction Sites, Donate

Curb Appeal – Invite Them In

Clear Entry And Pathways
Tidy Garden And Driveway
Mend Or Paint Fences
Prominent House Number
Working Doorbell, Plants Or Flowers

CHAPTER 4: ESTABLISHING THE ASKING PRICE

Major Pricing Considerations

First Price Your Best Price
Pricing Too High
Pricing Too Low

Price Subject To Market

Top Agent's Analysis

Comparative Market Analysis (CMA)

Similar Homes Sold

Local Competition

Failed Listings

Price/Days On Market

List Price vs Sale Price

Forming A Second Opinion

Appraisals

Inaccurate Estimate Tools To Avoid

Self Research

Self Analysis And Comparisons – What To Look For

Square Footage

Age And Condition

Bedrooms And Bathrooms

Amenities

Lot Size And Location

Marketing Conditions

Absorption Rate

Buyer's Market

Seller's Market

Transitional Market

Market Cycle

CHAPTER 5: LISTING AND SHOWING THE HOME

Multiple Listing Service (MLS) – Considerations

Maximum Exposure

Top Agent Listing Service

Brokers Locate Buyers

Active Marketing

Off-MLS Listings Or "Pocket Listings"

Showing The Property

Seller Flexibility

The Open House

Private Showings

Lock Box Showings

Maintain Staged Condition

CHAPTER 6: MANAGING AND SETTLING THE OFFER

Receiving The Offer

The Bid Price

Ability To Pay

Contingencies

Responding To The Offer

Accept The Offer

Reject The Offer

Counter The Offer

Negotiations

"Hardball" Techniques

Low-ball Offers

Bidding Wars

Speed Things Up

Closing The Deal

Exit Strategy

Full Disclosure

Sales Contract

"Escrow" Agent: Settlement And Transfer

"Closing Costs"

Closing Date

Moving Date: Make A Checklist

Moving Day – Considerations

Packing Tips: Stickers

Moving Van

New Insurance Coverage

Safety: Doors, Windows, Locks, Smoke Alarms

Unpack And Relax: Security And Success

Contents

Introduction

Chapter 1: Making The Decision To Sell – Important Considerations

Chapter 2: Considering Assistance As A First Time Home Seller

Chapter 3: Preparing The Home For Sale – First Impressions

Chapter 4: Establishing The Asking Price

Chapter 5: Listing And Showing The Home

Chapter 6: Managing and Settling The Offer

Conclusion

Bonus: Five Common Mistakes to Avoid When Selling a Home

Introduction

In today's forever-changing world, the real estate market can be a confusing place to navigate for any person, let alone the average first-time home seller. In real estate, there are certain measures one must take in order to succeed and to later, an aspiration of every home seller, emerge financially sound. Selling a house does not guarantee profit, but carrying out the steps outlined in this book will give you the highest chances of making your dreams a reality.

Every market is different and, existing within a digital world connected every second of every day, the world of buyers has evolved from what it used to be. You are about to discover the secrets to maximize your potential to succeed and to advance through each process of selling a house with comfort in the fact that you have taken every preparation necessary. This is not the same age we used to live in. Putting up a "For Sale" sign and posters is not enough.

When selling a home, one small mistake can ultimately end up costing that home owner thousands of dollars. There are legal obligations and necessary precautions to make when selling a house. Being aware of such extremities will save you valuable amounts of time and money, along with unnecessary legal disputes and last-minute hurdles. So how will you know how to do everything the right way? What constitutes the right way if it is subject to constant change? You have to know who to talk to. You will soon learn how to gain the upper hand in all aspects of every process of selling a home, from preparing your home for new owners to finding the best professional guidance possible to assist you in realizing your goals. The real estate market may change, but knowing the right routes to take and what tools to implement will never change as long as there are people willing to learn.

Knowing how things work and how things change over time is vital to succeeding in most of life's proceedings. If you are able to open your mind and follow directions, you are able to sell a home. This guide will teach you everything you need to know about the selling process and the transformation of your home into, essentially, an entirely new dwelling more fit to reel in buyers. Are you wondering where to begin? What should you put away and what should you keep out? Do you have to replace everything? What details do you need to invest in the most?

Your mind is swimming with questions and worries, all of which are steering you into a cloud of doubt. Before you start doubting yourself, know that as long as you can read these words, you can renovate your home before the sale while keeping a budget in mind.

While budgeting for renovations is important, there are other mandatory investments that aspiring sellers make the mistake of avoiding. Some homes need more work than others. Sometimes the biggest problems are the ones you never see. You have to spend money to make money in real estate, so the more corners are cut the more detrimental the outcome can be. Closing that deal and meeting your goals to turn the maximum profit for your home can be a daunting task, but with a strong plan of action under your sleeve there can be a happy ending to this story.

Ultimately, you will be the one to write your story in all facets of life. Your chances of success will mirror your efforts every step of the way. Everyone needs help, but many people have forgotten how important it is to ask. Our highest ambitions are as obtainable as we make them.

Often times we miss out completely until a new person with a fresh perspective is willing open our eyes. This is where you will find the fresh perspective you need to sell your home. Triumph is never guaranteed, but having a source like this to organize and augment such a paramount objective is the best way to proceed. You will be able to move forward with confidence while handling your largest financial asset. You are capable of realizing your dreams and, though it may seem insurmountable, your vision of securing the financial freedom needed to start the next chapter in your life is about to be unraveled.

Chapter 1: Making The Decision To Sell – Important Considerations

There are many reasons people choose the permanent solution of selling their homes. Some have too much or too little space to suit their needs, while others feel the need to relocate to be closer to family or friends. Facing financial turmoils and clearing debts are more pressing reasons many find themselves choosing to sell. Sadly, one of the most common reasons is divorce or the breakup of a relationship. Couples find themselves boggled down with attachments to their former partners and therefore need to sell in order to move on with their lives. Perhaps a person's spouse has passed away and that person wants to downsize or has inherited a property to sell for cash. This is known as bereavement. Some people are in very poor health and must opt to sell their homes because it is no longer suitable for them to live independently. Repossession is another reason a person may decide to sell, faced with the peril of clearing the debts they owe. Houses are not all made to last and many overwhelmed home owners find themselves burdened with devastating repairs. They simply have no way to fund the expense, let alone face the upheaval process.

All around the world, people are pushed by happenstance to do things they would never resort to otherwise. When facing the choice of selling your most precious financial asset, swelling emotions can narrow your view of the situation. Sometimes you can only make sense of the most obvious option that shoves its way into your mind. Before making a major life decision like selling your home, or any major decision for that matter, you have to consider all of the alternatives at your disposal. Rarely is there only one solution to a given problem and the following examples will prove so.

Here are some possible alternatives relevant to their corresponding situations to further support the importance of researching every available resource. If too little space is the issue, consider borrowing more in order to extend your current home. Try expanding out into the garden, down into the basement, or up into the loft space. If too much space is the issue, consider the financial benefits of renting out a room or even multiple rooms. The flip side is that you will have to be cautious and therefore selective about the individuals you allow to live under the same roof. Try to rent to people you already know you are compatible with. When meeting a new potential roommate, never appear weak minded or emotional. Crooks will use every vulnerability against you once they spot obvious signs of insecurity. If you emit confidence and portray a person not to be messed with, crooks will be more reluctant. There is a flip side to everything, but becoming a good judge of character is a life skill to take with you after the renting experience.

If relocation is necessary, consider keeping your home and renting it out. You may be able to obtain a "buy to let" mortgage or, if your current house is mortgaged, your lender may be happy to allow you to rent out, though usually at a slightly higher interest rate. Similarly, if you have inherited a property this might be a desirable option. It is important to remember that, in addition to your mortgage provider (if applicable), you will need to inform your buildings and contents insurer if you make the decision to rent out your home.

If you are having financial difficulties, consider changing your mortgage, such as extending your current term to lower your monthly payments, or remortgage to release some equity in your home so you can borrow a little more. Talk to your lender and think cautiously before changing your mortgage. Be certain that if you decide to increase your mortgage that you will be able to afford the monthly repayments. If you can, renting out a room can be a helpful accommodation here as well, but keep in mind that any rent you collect may be taxable depending on how much you receive.

For the elderly, having to move can be a detrimental loss. Luckily, if you are older, a lifetime mortgage could be the answer to your prayers. A lifetime mortgage is a certain kind of equity release loan based upon the value of your house. It allows those eligible to receive a lump sum or a regular income, but not without the stipulation of paying interest on the additional loan which is later added to the original loan amount. You still own your home and the loan is eventually repaid when your house is sold in the future. Keep in mind, however, that the interest accumulated is compounding, which means interest on the previous years' interest. There is a risk that the loan could grow to exceed the value of the house. However, any extra value derived from the property after being sold is paid to the appropriate heirs in the event of that person's death. Always know the specifications before choosing any alternative course of action.

A home reversion loan is another alternative some may find suitable. This allows you to sell all or part of your home to a company in exchange for a lump sum of cash, a regular income, or even both. While under a set lease, you retain the right to live in your home peacefully until the day you die. Usually, you can choose to sell between 25% and 100% of your property, but the amount you receive in return will be considerably less than that of the market value. The amount will depend on your age because the older you are, the more you receive. A beneficial proposal for those unable to uproot and sell through the market.

Some people have the option of "house-swapping" or "part-exchanging". Today, millions of people are all interconnected via the Internet. An endless stream of information and networking connects people from all corners of the world, allowing new possibilities the chance to uproot and expand. There are swapping websites that specialize in bringing people together who are willing to participate in this interesting way to avoid getting caught in a chain or paying estate agency fees. Technology continues to provide us with more innovative ideas as we strive to solve all of life's problems, from opening a bottle of wine to closing the sale of a home.

Now can you start to see why it is so important to do your research and to discover what options pertain to your own happenstance? These alternatives only skim the surface as a reminder of the magnitude of information and reliable services available to suit your needs. You are not alone in this fight and you have the ability to learn the techniques to come out on top. So now that you know what tools exist to help you make a definite decision, are you ready to start the process of selling your home? It will involve hard work and a willingness to follow the provided guidelines vital to success.

So you have decided to sell your home. This is not a task that can be done by yourself. So where do you begin? Before you thrust the gear into full throttle, there are some things you need to be sure about.

Timing is a good place to start. If you are not pressed to sell immediately, you can choose to sell when demand is high to give your property the best chance on the market. Typically, demand is high in Spring, early Summer, and Autumn. If possible, avoid the middle of Summer and the holiday seasons in Winter.

Take the time to soak in the wider picture. Again, this

will mean doing your own research to see what is happening in the housing market, both nationally and locally. Take note of what other sellers are doing and study top dollar houses recently sold on the market. Be aware of interest rates and the attitudes of current lenders.

Thoroughly research what is happening locally. Too many "For Sale" signs cluttering your area can ultimately put off potential buyers and drive house prices down. With luck, you may live in a location that appears immune to national trends and has a consistently buoyant market. Though this will not always be the case, you still hold the power to sway the odds in your favor. You will have to decide whether or not you want to invest in another home. The market will tell you if buying another house is plausible.

If you plan on buying and selling, a strategy most home owners find ideal, you have three main options: buy and sell at the same time, sell first, or buy first. Each will effectively generate a different outcome with different concerns. Timing is an important consideration in the application of any one of these options.

The first and most common scenario is to buy and sell at the same time. Whether you can manage to sell your current house or acquire the home of your dreams first is often a matter of planning and preparation. With a bit of luck, it can be done, but keep in mind that it can be stressful trying to sell and buy at once. Once you have found the house you want, you are going to want to step it up a notch and speed up your sale.

The second option is to sell first. This will allow you to be in a stronger negotiating position when you get around to buying, seeing as you will be chain free and have a clear idea about what price you can afford to offer. However, remember that you may end up having to rent an apartment, or other lodgings, while you are on the hunt for your new property. You may have to move twice and deal with storage payments, as all of your possessions will need to be kept safe while you sort everything out. Remember that prices may rise in the meantime. If renting is something you are unwilling or unable to do, you have the option of specifying to buyers that you will only accept an offer under the condition that you are able to find a suitable place to buy. This will involve delicate negotiation skills.

The third scenario is to buy first. This can lead to being put under a lot of pressure to sell your home quickly. You want to avoid the sheer expense of owning two homes at the same time and having a bridging loan to pay. Most lenders will refuse to give you a mortgage on your new home unless the other is being sold or you can prove you have the capability to keep up with both mortgages. For most people, one mortgage is enough, so this option is not the most ideal to the majority of home owners.

Be sure to budget for your sale and see where you stand. The costs associated with closing a deal alone are great, so renovating and repairing your home before the sale will require precise budgeting. Do not fret about the details now because this guide is about to explore the secrets to the least expensive, most appealing secrets to draw in buyers with a completely transformed home. For now, here is something to consider first on your journey to flip and sell a home while saving money.

All sellers are required by law to get an EPC. This stands for Energy Performance Certificate. An EPC shows you exactly how much energy a building uses. This helps home owners lower their energy bills and live more comfortably by making their homes more energy efficient. You must contact an accredited domestic energy assessor who will perform the assessment and provide the certificate. You can do this online at www.epcregister.com or through the phone book.

You have to make sure you know how much selling your home will cost you. Fees vary, but do not underestimate them because they tend to add up quickly. An Estate Agent's fee is payable when a real estate agent sells the property and contracts have been signed. Solicitors' fees are required as well. A solicitor is needed to guide you through the legal aspects of selling your home. This is called conveyancing. Costs vary, so always request a quote and make sure to ask if it is a fixed price because costs accumulate fast if there is a dispute or query on the paperwork. If you have chosen to buy and sell, some solicitors will provide you with a discount for handling the conveyancing for both.

You may also have to deal with current Lender's fees. Be sure to check for early repayment charges or any administrative fee payable provided you repay your mortgage. There will also be Removal costs which will vary depending on the amount you need to move, how far away you are moving, and whether you choose to use a professional firm. Depending on the circumstances, there can be Rental costs, bridging loans, and storage charges as well.

Generally, if you have lived in your home and it has always been your home in the time since you have owned it, you will not be forced to pay Capital Gains Tax on any revenue gained when you sell it. However, there might be some liability if the property you are selling is not your main residence or you have used part of it for business use. Business use such as using a room as your office, taking in lodgers, or letting out all or part of your home.

However, the profit you make upon selling your home produces capital gains, which are subject to capital gains taxes. Fortunately, a lot of sellers can avoid paying these capital gains taxes all together. Thanks to the Taxpayer Relief Act of 1997, you can exclude up to $250,000 in capital gains. Married couples can exclude up to $500,000 in capital gains. This means that if you bought a house for $100,000 and later sold it for $300,000, you would have $200,000 in capital gains completely tax free.

The final and most important consideration if you are going to sell your home for top dollar is hiring someone to assist you. Contrary to what others may say, selling a home is not something that should be done solo. Hiring a professional agent will give you the best chances of success. You will be able to sell your home quickly and have the most current tools and professional knowledge on your side.

Chapter 2: Considering Assistance As A First Time Home Seller

Homeowners make the mistake of assuming that by eliminating the agent, they will benefit by walking away with a greater percentage of the profit from the sale. This is not always how things turn out. When you list a property on your own, without the help of a real estate agent, it is referred to as "For Sale By Owner". The primary intention is to eliminate the middleman, the agent, and to avoid paying any real estate commission.

Unfortunately, FSBO listings have a fatal downfall right from the start. They immediately give off a certain vibe to home buyers. If you see a FSBO listing rather than the more common agent listing, you may automatically think "bargain" or "distressed sale". You may also think the seller is not serious and is just trying to see what they can get.

Aside from that, the seller who posts a FSBO listing may discover that many interested buyers are just bargain hunters passing through. Many are looking for a great deal because along the way they began associating the term "For Sale By Owner" with "bargain". This makes sense because it is a more seldom seen listing. FSBOs also have a failure rate of 85% to 95%. Buyers will take you more seriously when listing under an agent and your home will sell for significantly more. Statistics prove that selling your home with professional assistance will generate enough profit to pay for the commission, any agency fees, and still have extra money to put away.

The Internet makes it instantaneous for buyers to access every kind of property on the market, such as short sales and foreclosures. This creates massive competition. Realtors use certain gateways and connections via the Internet to put your property before the eyes of millions. A Top Realtor will have the tools to do this and much more.

Do not make the common mistake of thinking that all real estate agents are the same. In most places across the United States, there are several hundred or several thousand agents to choose from. Each real estate agent has different personal traits, different selling strategies, different ways to market houses, and different levels of skill. In most communities there are only a handful of top producing agents, a decent amount of average agents, and a lot of bad agents. In most regions, a few Top Realtors will end up taking 80% of the business while the other lesser agents are left with 20%. This only proves just how experienced they are at selling homes. Remember, your Top Agent also benefits when your home is sold for top dollar.

So how will you know how to choose a Top Producer amongst so many lesser prospects? It is extremely important to choose the "right" real estate agent. Unfortunately, it is very easy to obtain a real estate license. You have to know the right questions to ask. Interviewing is going to be your golden ticket to selecting a top producing agent. Swallow your shyness and try to think of yourself as a businessperson rather than a home owner. You are looking for the best candidate to conduct your business.

How long have you been selling real estate?

This is a very important interview question because, generally, more experience means more sales, along with the probability they have encountered a lot of different situations. However, there are new Realtors that can sell your home better than an agent with more than thirty years of experience.

Are you a full-time or a part-time Realtor?

Do not forget to ask this question because a true top producing Realtor will be full-time. Being a successful agent involves long hours and extreme dedication. Hiring a part-time real estate agent is not recommended because it is very likely that they will not have the time or availability to handle all of the aspects involved in the sale of your home.

What proven results do you possess? How many properties did you sell last year while representing a seller?

You want to ask these questions because many Realtors

work primarily with buyers just to trick you. Helping a buyer find a home and representing a seller with the sale of their home are two very different things. By asking how many homes they sold last year while representing sellers, you can figure out whether they primarily deal with buyers or sellers. Top Producers should possess a minimum ratio of 60/40. This means that sixty percent or more of their sales are representing sellers, while forty percent or less of their sales are representing buyers.

What was the average time from the listing date to the contract date concerning the sales?

When selling your home, especially for the first time, one of the worst fears is the possibility of your home staying on the market for a long period of time. During the interview, ask them how long it generally takes for their listings to reach an acceptable contract.

What was the average listing price to sale price ratio?

To no one's surprise, most sellers want top dollar for their homes. Asking a prospective Realtor about their average listing price to sale price ratio is very important. Do not make the common mistake of hiring a Realtor who "buys a listing". A Realtor who "buys a listing" will suggest listing a home for much higher than normal market value in order to secure a contract, then later continuously "beat up" a seller to lower the price. By asking this question in the interview, you significantly reduce the chance of this happening. A Top Producer should have an average listing price to sale price ratio of 95% or higher.

How many pending transactions do you currently possess?

This question will give you a great indication of a Realtor's level of success. If they only have one pending transaction, it is safe to assume that they are not a top agent. Top Producers should always have ten or more pending transactions.

What marketing and advertising "vehicles" do you use? Do you utilize the Internet for marketing your properties for sale?

There is no doubt that the Internet has had a huge impact on the real estate industry. Realtors who say the Internet is not a relevant part of real estate sales are either ignorant or unable to adapt and are therefore not being truthful. Do not forget to ask how they market their homes for sale online.

Do you have your own website that will come up in search results?

Seeing as there are far too many agents who do not have their own website, it is very important that the right agent has a their own high ranking website. Their website should rank on the first page, or at the very least the first couple pages.

Do you have your own real estate blog?

Blogs today are quite popular in many industries and the real estate industry is no exception. Realtors use blogs to write about questions frequently asked by buyers and sellers, current real estate topics, and homes they are selling.

Do you use social media?

Facebook, Twitter, Pinterest, and Instagram are all social media sites. During the interview, asking the Realtor what social media sites they utilize tells you whether or not they understand the importance of exposure when selling their client's home. The aim is to provide as much exposure as possible and this gives them an edge over other agents who are not active on social media.

What camera do you use when taking pictures of the homes you sell?

Properties that have terrible photos have a poor chance of selling. You want a Realtor who has the ability to take quality photos or has a professional photographer on stand by. They should have a high quality camera with high quality lenses, not a digital one.

What methods do you use to calculate the listing price of the homes you sell?

Realtors use different methods to price homes. Any

prospective Realtor should be able to provide an example of a comparative market analysis (CMA) for you to view. Pay attention to the amount of detail used in their analysis to determine how much time and effort they spend on pricing their homes.

Do you have testimonials from past sellers whose homes you sold?

This is not an unreasonable request. Most Top Producers will have testimonials on hand or on their website. If possible, ask if you can contact any past clients to speak with them directly about their experience.

Which methods do you use to communicate with your sellers and how often?

Lack of communication is a big issue for both sellers and buyers. Find out how frequently they touch base with their sellers so you know what to expect in the future.

How much do you charge for your services?

Because commission is negotiable, it is important to ask prospects what percentage they require. Just because one agent may offer less than another does not mean you are getting a deal. You could be costing yourself a lot of money. Top Producers should be able to justify their commission fees.

Are there penalties for canceling a contract?

Most of time, there are penalties for the early cancellation of a contract. Ask if the Realtor will enforce the penalty. A Top Realtor will have the confidence necessary to get your home sold, so a penalty for an early termination should not be an issue.

Make sure you understand what type of contract you are signing and its length. There are three main types of listing agreement contracts: Open Listing, Exclusive Agency Listing, and Exclusive Right-to-Sell Listing. The best choice for you depends on your willingness to handle certain home selling duties and the real estate market climate.

An "Open Listing" contract involves the use of multiple agents in order to sell the property and get it off the market. The agent that sells the home collects the commission. An "Exclusive Agency Listing" contract means that a specified agent earns the commission if the home sells within a specified number of months, no matter how a buyer is found. An "Exclusive Right-to-Sell Listing" agreement states that the seller must pay the brokerage a commission if, by the expiration date specified, the property is sold, regardless of whether the buyer is found through the agency or not. Even if the seller obtains the buyer themselves, the brokerage still receives a commission.

Asking these interview questions will give you the best

chances at fetching top price for your home. You will be able to judge quickly whether or not you are dealing with a Top Agent or an incompetent bungler. If you feel you want to prepare yourself further, research more interview questions you can ask. There is no such thing as a stupid question. A true agent will be happy to answer any questions you have, from start to finish.

What should you expect from your real estate agent during the sale process? A successful real estate agent should possess certain qualities. These traits separate the top agents from the amateur agents, and having high expectations is key to prevent yourself from being swindled. Show them that you will not be taken for a fool.

Honesty is the first and most important trait. Even though Realtors have their own code of ethics to abide by, not all agents tell the truth. If an agent is unable to provide any testimonials or previous clients' contact information upon your request, they are not being honest with you and they do not have experience.

Professionalism is a trait most sellers assume all agents have, but this is not the case. What actions prove that a real estate agent possesses professionalism? The most obvious sign is a polished image. Realtors should appear well dressed and properly groomed. Buyers will not take agents who wear jeans and sneakers seriously. Being a professional also means respecting other's time and being punctual.

Negotiating skills are very important. The job of a Realtor representing a seller is to get the most money for their client's home in the least amount of time. The right candidate should know what to say to a buyer's representative. They should also know not to send a counter offer from their client to the buyer's agent without any discussion. This is unacceptable, as they are supposed to be the voice of the seller.

Creativity is a great quality for a real estate agent to have, indicating their level of adaptability and wit. No two homes are exactly the same, so agents need to know which selling strategies to apply. Property descriptions, photo angles, and writing advertisements are all things they must be creative with. This is where a lot of agents fall short. This trait ties in directly with experience and proven results. The more business an agent conducts, the better they are at handling specific situations. These qualities should earn any dedicated Top Producer a great reputation through their company, which is another attribute to assess. Always do your research every step of the way, as word of mouth will not be enough to ensure you have chosen the best candidate for the job.

The next step is the assessment of quality techniques. True professionals align themselves with other great professionals. It is crucial to find out what business connections and services they offer. Upon request, a Top Producer should be able to suggest other real estate attorneys and mortgage consultants for potential purchasers. They should be more than willing to tell you what relocation network they belong to, what movers they can suggest upon the sale of your home, and what preferred partners or vendors they can recommend.

The use of "cutting-edge" technology is extremely important. Ask about what technological tools they use when selling a property. Utilizing advanced technology allows real estate agents to be more efficient, providing them with more time to spend selling homes. Popular advances that help agents include tools such as digital signature software, iCloud, Dropbox, Evernote, and Buffer.
A comprehensive marketing plan is a paramount technique to consider.

Overpricing is a common mistake sellers make, and it is important to note that an overpriced home will not sell, even with the best marketing strategy. What does a comprehensive marketing plan entail? A real estate agent should use a mixture of both "older" and "newer" tactics in their marketing plan. "Older" tactics you should expect include television advertisements, newspaper articles, and direct mailings. "Newer" marketing tactics to expect include the use of their own personal website, personal blog, and social media profiles. A strong online presence is crucial, seeing as the majority of buyers start their search online.

You can take comfort in the fact that, upon hiring a Top Agent from an established agency, you are protected by a complaints process. This gives the agents incentive to please every client, seeing as doing an unsatisfactory job will hinder their reputation with the agency. Now that you know the right questions to ask and what to expect, you can confidently weed out the right agent to accomplish your goals as a first time home seller.

Chapter 3: Preparing The Home For Sale – First Impressions

Now that you have professional help, it is time to prepare your home for future showings. Your real estate agent will no doubt have an opinion on this subject, but you are about to learn everything you need to know to transform your home. Try to see your home from a buyer's perspective. You must ensure that your home is "show ready" to attract buyers willing to pay your asking price. To do this, improvements must be made. Making a good first impression is key.

First, tackle both minor and major repairs. Maintenance takes up a lot of time, but does not have to cost a lot of money. Clean out your gutters, re-grout tiles, replace light bulbs, fix leaky taps, polish wooden flooring, oil creaking hinges, and anything else in need of improving. This will give viewers the impression of a maintained, well-loved home.

If you want to make a great impression, "Staging" is going to be your best friend. Staging your home involves making a lot of changes, but there are ways to "paint a picture" without going overboard. The aim here it to simplify, rearrange, re-purpose, and "renovate", all while using mainly pieces that were there but were just improperly utilized. You want to create a neutral, updated environment that buyers can imagine themselves actually living in. The first thing to consider when painting a picture is the disadvantage of too many personal touches.

Who knew that taking down family photos and clearing off counter tops helps you achieve top dollar for your house? Family photos and personal items make people feel like they are invading your space. These are just two secrets to the art of staging. You can clean up, rearrange, and style your home to command top price. This means anything from putting excess books in storage to cleaning up moldy buildup in bathrooms to filling up bare spaces. The goal is to make your home clean, organized, and inviting so potential buyers can picture themselves moving in.

You want to de-personalize your home. If you want viewers to immediately envision themselves living in your home, "you" need to move out by removing personal things like CDs, DVDs, theme items, and so on. You may adore your deep purple walls but viewers prefer a blank canvas they can stamp their own personality on.

A great tip when staging your home is to replace mismatched pictures with chic, artistic photos, along with generally appealing art pieces to accent any bare walls. Be very considerate about placement. Look up examples of rooms staging experts have recreated on a budget. They will usually specify where they found expensive looking pieces for a bargain while re-purposing bigger items for a whole new look. Keep neutral colors, like black and brown, in mind while adding pops of color and texture. Fur pillows and area rugs are a great way to add texture in a room. Try placing a couple of decorative lanterns on the coffee table for a more modern appeal. A wonderful tip is to add touches that invoke an emotional response in buyers, such as placing a book by the arm chair or baking a fresh batch of chocolate chip cookies. If you are creative and do some research, you can stage your home without spending a lot of money.

Do not take on too many projects, but have fun making a home someone would want to live in. There are a lot of great low-cost projects and tips. Try painting the walls a warm, neutral shade. You can also add an accent wall by painting it two shades deeper or a complimentary color. Repaint cabinets and furniture as needed and replace cheaper items like knobs, light switch covers, and electrical outlets. Buy new neutral colored towels and shower curtains.

Lighting is also important. Try changing lampshades and replacing old light fixtures with colorful pendants. Also, it is important to choose light bulbs that have the right spectrum for a given space. Soft bulbs that emit a yellow or red undertone are best in "hanging out" areas such as the living room. Bright bulbs that emit blue undertones do well in "study" areas such as the office or library. New blinds and curtains add a charming finishing touch, along with molding, trim, and other accents.

Before listing your house for sale, getting a home inspection is absolutely essential. A pre-sale inspection will help you address any larger repairs you were unable to pinpoint so you can properly price and market your property. The inspector's report will give buyers the confidence they need to make an offer on your property. Fixing the issues will help you get a higher offer. Home inspections should be part of the preparation process. Too many sellers make the mistake of waiting until later to deal with the home inspection, risking lower offers and scaring away buyers.

When preparing your home, de-cluttering is an important process. Get rid of knick-knacks and clear out any bulk items, such as toys, newspapers, clutter, and so on. Rearrange to create a different flow throughout the house. The idea is to create the illusion of space. A secret technique to do this is the use of mirrors. Put two large decorative mirrors on opposing walls across from each other. The reflections create the feeling of a larger space while drawing in more light. If you have a "junk room", convert it to a tidy office or study.

Tackle the garage, shed, loft, underneath the stairs, cupboards, and kitchen units. When you are finished it should be apparent what each room is for. Open rooms and welcoming accents, such as a vase of flowers, may seem overly plain, but do not underestimate the value you are adding to your home just by clearing bulk.

You will want to put your bigger possessions, along with any other items you cannot bear to part with, away. You may want to consider renting a storage unit. Alternatively, you can opt to turn your clutter into cash by using online auction sites, such as eBay, or having a garage sale. If you are the giving type, charity shops welcome donations and many will pick up the items for you. You can also give family or friends anything you no longer need.

Now that you have de-cluttered, a good clean is required. Vacuuming, flicking a duster, and spraying air freshener is not enough. You are going to have to deep clean the house from top the bottom. Pay particular attention to the kitchen and bathrooms. Scrub grime and grout clean to make them sparkle. Move furniture, clean behind everything, wipe down the walls, clean the corners, wash windows on either side, and dust and polish everything. Make sure everything is spotless, including appliances like the oven and dishwasher.

The outside of your home is just as important at the inside. It is proven that buyers decide within the first six seconds whether or not they like a home. They are going to see the outside first, so make sure you consider curb appeal when making a strong first impression. It should be obvious how to enter your home. Each side of the doorway should welcome them through and into the threshold. Paint the front door a color that stands out against the greenery, like red, or buy a new one. Give the outside of the house a fresh coat of paint. Clear pathways, mow the lawn, tidy the garden and parking lot, repair and repaint the fencing, and make sure the house number is prominent and the doorbell works. Adding a few tubs of flowers or plants is a big plus point and you can take them with you when you move. Just do everything you can to get the home in excellent shape and be prepared to make some minor concessions at closing time.

If you are not decorative or creatively inclined, remember that your agent can recommend a plan of action to get your home "show ready". If you can manage to get creative and do your research, you can save a lot of money while at the same time adding thousands to your home's sale price. View other show homes online to give yourself an idea of how to present and market a house. Study examples posted by professional stagers from their portfolios. This will also show you what you are competing against and if you need to step up your game.

Chapter 4: Establishing The Asking Price

Your home's first price should be its best price. The number one reason a home does not sell is because it is incorrectly priced. When putting your home on the market, especially if you are living in a region where prices are increasing and buyers are competing for homes, it can be a tempting thought to list at a high price to see if you can get it. This is not a good idea. Sale prices are not based on the owner's needs. When an owner is determined to sell for $300,000 to gain $100,000 to buy their next home, buyers want to know if it is a reasonable price. If similar homes on the market are selling for $250,000, the owner will not be successful. Experienced Realtors will tell you that pricing your home appropriately from the start is critical to selling quickly and for the best price. Most successfully sold homes stay on the market for mere weeks.

Marketing statistics show that overpricing your home and then reducing the price repeatedly usually results in a much lower profit margin than you originally should have received. The longer a home stays on the market, the more discounted the price becomes. You have to price your home correctly. Many homeowners want to set their listing price based on what they originally paid for their home, the balance of their mortgage, or the profit they expect to make so that they can move into another home.

In reality, your home is only worth what the market will allow.

Price your home too high and risk buyers passing your property by or simply walking away without making an offer. Some sellers are tempted when selecting an agent to hire the one that suggests the highest price for their home, but this is a mistake. That agent is just telling them what they want to hear. When you price your home too high, you are helping sell other homes in your vicinity that are listed for less. After seeing your top dollar home, buyers may be tempted to get the better deal nearby, even if they liked your home better. A lot of buyers do their research, just as you do as a seller, and many will have a good idea of what homes in your neighborhood are worth..

Homes ultimately sell at a price the buyer is willing to pay and the seller is willing to accept. If a property is priced low, a strategy that involves less risk, the seller might potentially receive multiple offers to bring the price up to market value. Sellers can also lose tens of thousands of dollars if they set the price too low. Follow your expert's advice, but keep in mind that you will need to leave room for negotiation for when the time comes to close a deal. Some sellers price too high in order to leave room for negotiation and run the risk of being overlooked by buyers on a more strict budget. Then there is no one to negotiate with. A lot of buyers enjoy the negotiating process and can be smooth talkers. Other more solid buyers appreciate and respect a home priced just right.

Have realistic expectations of what your home will sell for, but remember to utilize your Top Agent to calculate the highest price possible in relation to the market.

It is standard practice for a real estate agent to visit and evaluate your home upon request. Your Realtor will be able to provide the best comparative market analysis and explain exactly how your home should be priced. Your property will have the best chances of selling quickly and for a higher price.

To further elaborate, a comparative market analysis (CMA) includes sales prices for similar homes nearby that have sold within the last month or so. Many Realtors also include prices for homes presently on the market to show you the competition, as well as homes taken off the market that were unable to be sold.

Other data Realtors use to determine a price range include how many days homes spent on the market at what price and the average difference between the listing prices and the sale prices on recently sold homes. The difference between the listing prices and the actual selling prices for homes in your region speaks volumes about the current real estate market. It is a strong indication of which direction the market is moving in. This will ultimately determine your asking price and whether you can get more than you originally anticipated or less. Remember that CMAs are not set in stone. Some agents will under value a home in hopes of creating demand. Others try to flatter clients with overly inflated estimates in order to get them to list but later suggest reducing the price. Conduct your own investigation so you know what to expect when your Realtor suggests a figure for your home upon further analysis.

If you want a second opinion, you can hire an impartial appraiser. An appraiser will help you pinpoint any updates you may have missed that could fetch you a better selling price. Valuating is not an exact science and every appraiser will have a different opinion. If you are selling to buyers who are getting a mortgage, which is the majority of buyers, the lender will need an appraisal. If comparable home sales over the past months and current market conditions do not support your listing price, then your buyer will not get the mortgage.

It is critical that first time home sellers avoid inaccurate ways to price a home, such as using the home's assessed value or using an online valuation estimate like Zillow's "Zestimates". It is impossible for an online website based out of a certain city to accurately establish the price of a home in a completely different region. Looking up the value of your home online can be confusing because each site may have a different estimate with no date to support how or why they chose that number. Online calculations may include short sales, bank owned sales, or homes not in the same condition. Values can vary greatly. When coming up with a listing price, you do not want to gamble or guess.

The only true way to get an idea of your home's worth and what the list price should be for yourself is to compare your home with other homes in the area. Take on a buyer's perspective when scoping out other houses for sale or that have recently sold. You can use Trulia to familiarize yourself with what nearby homes are listed for and selling for. Just be sure to think of the information you gather as a ballpark guide rather than an exact number. Before you head out the door to visit open houses and compare your home with the rest of the town, you need to know what to look for.

Every house is different, so analyzing comparisons will require some detective work. As a first time home seller formulating your own opinion, you will want to take note of what similar homes have that yours does not, as well as what your home has that others lack. Take note of square footage, as this is important to most buyers. When it comes to pricing, the bigger the house, the bigger the price tag. Note age and condition as well. Newer homes do not necessarily sell for more, but condition relative to age tends to factor into the price. Try to stay within a five-year range when comparing your home with others. The condition of a house can make or break a deal, so you want pay attention to other homes' upgrades to assess how they affect value. Note all of the bedrooms and bathrooms in your home. The number of bedrooms and baths, and where they are located within the home, can have a radical affect on the price. Also, pay special attention to amenities. The more perks you have, the better. Walk-in closets, a gourmet kitchen, and an existing pool or spa add to the value of your home. Be sure to take note of lot size, as the precise acreage of your land correlates to price. Stay within 0.5 acres when you compare your lot with others.

Location is another notable, multifaceted factor to assess. Location relates to your state, city, neighborhood, and the placement of your house on the street. Note whether it faces toward any eyesores or busy traffic intersections. Does it have a nice view? Is there a freeway nearby that produces noise, or is there a tranquil lake behind it to enjoy? You will want to take all of these location nuances into consideration.

While compiling your own research, just observing what homes are not selling at what price will be a great help in determining your own home's approximate worth. You will be better prepared to discuss the analysis and valuation of your home with a professional. You will be more informed and more confident in your ability to follow all of the proceedings your real estate agent will lead you through when establishing an accurate representation of your home's value.

Your Realtor can help you estimate who might want to buy your property and what else those buyers are looking at so you can compare your price against the competition. A knowledgeable Realtor will be able to factor in all of these obstacles in the context of your local market conditions, including whether it is a "buyer's market" or "seller's market" and whether house prices are rising or falling. You can do your research on the side, but listen to your expert's advice so your transaction is more likely to run smoothly and quickly from the beginning. If you have hired a Top Producer, you can take comfort in the fact that you are in the best hands of the business.

Most people have heard of the terms "buyer's market" and "seller's market", but few actually know what they mean and how they are determined. There are many factors that affect the real estate market, such as interest rates, investment growth, legislative changes, employment, and new construction. All of these factors influence the market and its behavior in some way or another.

A market's absorption rate is the best way to determine whether a particular area is functioning as a buyer's market or a seller's market. The absorption rate is the rate at which homes sell in a given province. The higher the absorption rate, the faster properties are selling. Absorption rate is calculated by dividing the number of homes that have sold in the past month by the total number of homes listed for sale at the end of the month. If a region contains homes within two different price margins, you can determine the absorption rate specifically for homes within your price range. For example, if 6 properties sell in November for between $300,000 and $500,000, and 30 are still for sale at the close of the month, the absorption rate is 6/30, or 20%. If only 1 property sells and 15 remain, the absorption rate is 1/15, or 6%. This is the best method used amongst professionals to decide what kind market a house will be up against. Realtors refer to market types in terms according to who holds the advantage and how real estate is behaving.

A buyer's market is one in which there are more sellers and homes up for sale than there are buyers. Supply is greater than demand, so homes will have lower prices that are more attractive to buyers. This could be the result of high unemployment rates, fear of interest rate increases, or other factors that make people think twice about purchasing their first house or upgrading to a larger home. Buyers have the advantage in this market setting because they can typically take their time and explore all available options before buying. Buyers have more options because sellers are anxious to make a deal. Generally, prices tend to fall in a buyer's market. An absorption rate of 20% or lower is usually deemed a buyer's market seeing as homes sell relatively slow and the number of months of supply is high.

In a seller's market, there are more buyers than there are homes for sale. Seeing as supply is less than demand, homes will have higher prices that are more desirable for sellers. The factors at play could be consistently low interest rates, high employment rates, or legislative changes that make it easier to purchase property. These conditions influence buyers to think it is a great time to invest in buying a home. The seller has the advantage is a seller's market. Typically, house prices will increase as buyers are quick to make an offer in order to secure the property. Sometimes buyers will compete or bid for a property, raising the price above the seller's expectations.

An absorption rate of 20% or higher is typically deemed a seller's market since homes tend to sell quickly and the number of months of supply is low.

Buying a home in a seller's market is a competitive affair. Multiple offers made on the same house are not uncommon. Many of these offers may be above the asking price. Buyers can improve their negotiating position by having their finances in order, getting pre-approved for a mortgage, being prepared to act swiftly, and making a strong first offer. However, they are still at the mercy of the market's escalating prices and bidding wars.

If your home is for sale in a seller's market, this is the ideal time to reap the rewards of price appreciation. Generally, you will have more leverage in the negotiation process. However, keep in mind that, regardless of having a more favorable position in the market, it would be wise to be realistic and remain open-minded when negotiating. A seller's market does not automatically mean that you will get full price, immediate sale, agreement to all terms, or instant satisfaction.

A "transitional market" is one in which marketing conditions do not necessarily favor buyers or sellers. A transitional period occurs between moves toward either a buyers' market or sellers' market. The market does not change overnight. There is a transitional period in between while housing supply and demand are approximately equal and pricing generally stabilizes.

A market cycle can last for any given length of time. Market conditions can last months and sometimes even years. It all depends on the driving forces behind the transition. Even for the best experts, predicting the timing and duration of changes is a big challenge. The only thing that is certain is that sooner or later the housing market will change. Neither parties can have the upper hand all the time, but accepting that change is inevitable and knowing what market you are selling in will give you an informed advantage as you price your home for the big sale.

Chapter 5: Listing And Showing The Home

After much deliberation, you have chosen to sell through a top producing agent and you have "staged" your home on a budget to maximize its worth and showing potential. You have agreed upon the best marketing strategy set by your Realtor according to local supply and demand, and you have established an appropriate price for your property. You are finally ready to list. You will need help if you are going to gain the exposure you need while listing to achieve a successful sale as a first time home seller.

Top Agents use listing services to gain maximum exposure for their clients' properties. Your Top Producer will likely use a Multiple Listing Service (MLS). More than 80% of homes that sell are listed on their local Multiple Listing Service. As a home seller, the MLS gives you a lot more exposure to buyers. It is the best and most efficient way to list your home. Many buyers use real estate agents that also use the MLS as their main tool to locate homes for their buyers. If you are amongst the one in five sellers who choose not to sell through the MLS, you are crippling your odds of a successful sale within a desirable time frame.

Once you list on MLS, Realtors throughout the area are notified directly about your property and can start bringing prospects to you. Every real estate agent in your vicinity will be able to see your home when you list on the MLS. If you choose this route, you will dramatically increase your chances of selling quickly. Keep in mind that if an agent on the MLS is able to help you find a buyer, you will have to pay a buyer's agent commission, which is typically 2% or 3%.

The "MLS" is the database owned by various real estate agents and their regional trade associations. MLS systems are the primary channel used amongst agents and brokerages to publicize listings. Every day, new listings are entered in the database and dispersed to all subscribing agents and services. Active marketing for your home through the MLS usually includes open houses, agent tours, and the inclusion of your property in the MLS's download to other real estate sites regularly used to search for properties.

Listings that are marketed without the benefit of the MLS are called "off-MLS listings", or "pocket listings". An off-MLS listing, as the term suggests, is marketed by a single agent to one or two select potential buyers. The marketing pool can be so shallow that, in some cases, other agents working for the same brokerage may be completely unaware that a fellow agent has an off-MLS listing.

Many real estate professionals believe that off-MLS listings are not in the best interest of the property owner. These listings do not get the exposure that properties on the MLS do, which can significantly decrease the number of offers those sellers will receive. So why do home sellers agree to do this? Some off-MLS listings are requested by people who need to maintain their privacy or want to limit the exposure of their property to a particular individual or individuals with the financial means to purchase. This includes judges, prosecutors, celebrities, and so on. As a first time home seller, you will want to list your property on the local MLS to ensure it receives maximum exposure on multiple websites.

Once your Realtor has listed your home in the database, people will want to view your home. Showings for your property are essential to the selling process. Your Realtor will handle appointments upon your request, so have a drop box for a key ready. It is time to show off all your hard work, but keep the following considerations in mind.

As a seller, you do not want to make the common mistake of creating restrictions on when your home can be shown. You need to be flexible, even if it is inconvenient. Focus on the prize and be sure to clean and maintain your house before every visit. Buyers who want to view your home are going to contact your agent and expect to see it immediately. Make your home available every hour of the day. Otherwise, within a few days, prospective buyers will lose interest in your home and move on to another one. Also, studies show that buyers feel more comfortable and linger more when homeowners are not present during showings. Be sure to leave the house when buyers visit and let your agent do your smooth talking for you.

When presenting your home, keep in mind the main methods for showing, which include open houses, private showings, and lock box showings. Open houses are great for sellers because they can be assured that a good number of buyers can view the property, sometimes within a two or three-hour period. Open houses are open to anyone.

A buyer who attends your open house and likes your property may want to see it again privately. This is known as a private showing, which can be challenging for some sellers who are not maintaining the home's "staged" appearance. Try to reserve private showings for serious prospects who need more time to take a closer look. They are making a huge decision, so it is important they are able to investigate without feeling rushed.

Some sellers work during the day or their home for sale is vacant, which can make showing the home much easier. To make things easier for everyone involved, a lock box containing the house key should be installed on the front door. Agents can then use their local MLS key to open the lock box as needed. This is ideal for both the buyer and seller in terms of availability.

Homeowners who are serious about selling their homes should be ready for anything. Always keep your home neat and tidy in its "staged" condition. You want to make a good impression every time a potential buyer steps through the door. Buyers may have ideas for improvements, so inform your Realtor that you are open to suggestions. Showings in general, especially private showings, may be inconvenient, but they may also lead to offers.

Chapter 6: Managing and Settling The Offer

Every strategy you have implemented thus far in this guide has been leading up to this moment. This is the moment you have been waiting for. You have a purchase offer on your property. Should you accept the offer? Deciding on an offer and setting the terms of the settlement are often the hardest parts of the selling process, but they are also the most exciting. You may choose to accept an offer, reject it, or make a counteroffer. When you receive a buyer's offer, the buyer will submit a purchase agreement including some earnest money—a partial down payment—which is refundable if you decline. The purchase agreement will include the price being offered, how the buyer will pay for the property, and the date the transaction will be completed. Upon receiving an offer, you will want to review the following before making a decision.

The bid price. If the bid price is within 3% to 5% of you asking price, you have a great offer. Most agents will urge you to consider accepting such a great offer, unless you have another prospect that might make a higher bid. A buyer's ability to pay is essential. A buyer or their Realtor should be able to provide you with a lender qualification letter that proves the buyer is qualified to pay for the home.

Contingencies are another factor up for review. If a buyer makes an offer dependent on the sale of his or her own home, or based on something in your house that needs fixing, it is up to you to decide if the buyer is being unrealistic. It is possible for buyer to be particular and ask for too much, so weigh the contingencies against the bid price.

As a seller, you may want to consider adding your own contingencies. Consider loan approval. Sometimes purchase agreements can be made based on the buyer being approved for a loan within a designated time frame. Usually they have thirty days or less. If you decide that you want to help finance the home, put all of the precise terms of your contract in writing.

Also, do not forget the contingency of property. Putting all agreements that involve the property in writing benefits both the buyer and seller. To elaborate, if the buyer stipulates that they will only buy the property if the roof is repaired or the furniture comes with it, you should include this is the agreement. Be sure to include the highest price you have agreed to pay for repairs in the purchase agreement.

Now that you know what factors to consider, how you choose to handle your offer is important. So how do you respond? How do you protect your interests without sending buyers running for the hills? The first thing to remember is that all offers are good due to the fact that a buyer has chosen your home over all others on the market. Any offer should be taken as an extreme compliment, regardless of how high or low it might be. The hard part is deciding if you should accept the offer.

As a seller, you always have three main options. First, you can accept the offer. Second, you can reject the offer, which effectively tells the buyer off. Or third, you can counteroffer. Many sellers will instinctively want to counter all offers. Wise sellers are more cautious when making this decision.

Many sellers think that making a counteroffer is a natural part of negotiation procedure during the sale process, but what many fail to realize is that they are actually rejecting the buyer's offer and then presenting a new one in its place. The problem with this is, the second you give the buyer a chance to pause and reconsider their proposal, you run the risk of losing the buyer entirely. Successful sellers have learned to ask themselves if it will be worth it to counteroffer. In many cases, the risk is simply not worth the reward.

If you are forced to make a counteroffer, consider the following negotiation strategies. Strategy consideration number one is attempting to put yourself in the buyer's shoes. Try to understand the buyer's position. A negotiation is never a one way street because there are always different perspectives involved. In order to reach the point of a successful sale, both parties must feel that they are receiving a good value. Learn as much about the buyer as you can, including their background and their reasons for making their initial offer. By doing this, you may be able to find a common ground that can lead to a smooth sale.

The second strategy is to use the "give and take" technique. When making a counteroffer, think in terms of what you want and what you might be willing to sacrifice in order to make the sale happen. For instance, if you are asking for a higher price, can you help the buyer pay for their closing costs or maybe pay points to help them obtain lower payments? Unwilling first time sellers often make the mistake of not compromising, which costs them the sale in the end.

Thirdly and lastly, emphasize the positives. When you write your counteroffer, you may want to emphasize the areas that you do agree on before you start requesting modifications. Point out all of the details of the original offer you find acceptable. This might include the closing date, the possession date, the price, the down payment, the financing type, contingencies, inclusions and exclusions, or even something as simple as the amount of the earnest money deposit.

Take the time to evaluate each offer and create a negotiating strategy with the help of your real estate agent. An unemotional analysis of the market and of your needs as a seller will put you far ahead of your competition. Your Top Agent will be able to negotiate on your behalf and proceed with a strategy that you approve of, relieving you of unneeded stress if things heat up. There are many opinions out there, so come up with your own negotiation strategy.

Do not make the mistake of letting your ego get in the way when negotiating. Too many sellers take the process personally and lose out on creating a win-win scenario. It is a business transaction, so keeping your ego out of the equation and putting your head back into it is absolutely mandatory for success.

Selling your house is most likely one of the largest financial transactions you will undertake in your lifetime. The decisions you make when agreeing upon a price with a buyer will have a great impact on how much money you actually walk away with. If you want a more cut-throat strategy, discuss it with your Realtor and see if it would be a good idea based on the kind of buyers you are dealing with. Here are some "hardball" negotiating techniques that will help you achieve top dollar for your home in any market.

Counteroffer at your listing price. As a seller, you probably will not want to agree to a potential buyer's initial offer on your house. Buyers usually expect a back-and-forth negotiation, so their initial offer is almost always lower than what they are actually willing to pay and lower than your listing price.

At this point, most sellers will counteroffer with a price that is below their listing price because they are afraid of the sale slipping through their fingers. They want to seem flexible and open to negotiation in order to seal a deal. This strategy works in terms of getting the property sold, but it is not necessarily the best way to get the highest price, which is your goal as a first time home seller.

Instead of dropping your initial price to get closer to the buyer's bid, counter at your list price. A buyer who is serious about purchasing will stay engaged and come back with a higher bid. Assuming you have priced your home appropriately from the start, countering at your list price says that you know what your house is worth and that you have every intention of getting the money you deserve.

Buyers may be surprised at this strategy and some will be turned off by your unwillingness to cooperate and walk away. However, you will also avoid wasting your time on the buyers who try to low-ball sellers, and who are not so interested in buying your house as they are in getting a deal.

If you really want to play hardball, you can try a negotiation tactic that is more extreme than countering at your list price. Reject the buyer's offer and do not counteroffer at all. To keep them in the game, you then request that they submit another offer. If they are truly interested and you have not turned them off, they will. This strategy sends a much stronger message that you know your property is worth what you are asking for. If the buyer does resubmit, they will have to make a better offer.

Additionally, if you do not counter, you are not tied down or locked into a negotiation with a specific buyer, and you can accept a higher bid if it comes along. For the buyer, knowing that others could come along and make better offers at any moment creates pressure to submit a competitive offer quickly, especially if they really want the house. This strategy can be very effective if house has only been on the market for a short period or if you have an open house approaching.

Another strategy is to hold off all offers until a certain date to try to create a bidding war. After the home is on the market and available to be shown, schedule an open house for a few days later. Refuse to accept any offers until after the initial open house is over. Potential buyers will assume they are dealing with real competition and may place higher bids as a result. You might only get a single offer, but the buyer is unaware of that. On the flip side, if you get multiple offers, you can return to the top bidders and ask for their highest and best offers.

A good tactic is to put an expiration date and time on your counteroffer. When a buyer submits a bid you do not wish to accept, you counter their offer. You are then involved in a legally binding negotiation with that person, so you are not allowed to accept a better offer if it comes up. In the interest of selling your home as quickly as possible, consider assigning a short expiration date to your counteroffer. This method compels the buyer to make a decision so that you can either get your house under contract or move on.

You do not want to make the deadline so short that the buyers are turned off, but consider making it shorter than the typical time frame specified in your state's standard real estate contract. So, if the default expiration is four days, you might want to shorten it to two or three days.

Sellers must make fast decisions if they hope to close a deal quickly. While the counteroffer is outstanding, your property is effectively off the market. Many buyers will not place an offer when they see another negotiation is underway. If the deal falls through, you have added time to the number of days your property has sat on the market. The more days a home sits on the market, the less desirable it appears. It is therefore more likely that you will have to lower your asking price to reel in a buyer.

Agree to pay the buyer's closing costs, but increase the purchase price. It seems to have become standard practice for buyers to request that the seller pay their closing costs. These fees generally add up to about 3% of the purchase price, covering what seems to be a lot of frivolous charges. Buyers will often feel financially drained from having to come up with a down payment, moving expenses, redecorating costs, and furniture, so dealing with closing costs becomes unappealing. Some buyers cannot even afford to close the deal at all without the seller's assistance for closing costs.

While a lot of buyers do not have or do not want to spend extra money up front to get into the home, they can often afford to borrow a little more. If you decide to help them with closing costs, the sale may be more likely to proceed.

When a buyer submits a bid and then asks you to pay their closing fees, counter with a willingness to pay but only at a higher purchase price, even if that means going above your listing price. Buyers often forget that when they ask the seller to pay their closing costs, the are effectively decreasing the home's sale price. As a seller, you will be able to see the bottom line clearly.

You can raise your asking price by enough to still get as much as your list price after paying the buyer's closing fees. For example, say your listing price is $200,000. If the buyer offers $190,000 with $6,000 toward closing costs, you would counter with an offer between $196,000 with $6,000 for closing and $206,000 with $6,000 for closing. The only catch is that the price plus any closing costs must be supported when the house is appraised. Otherwise, you will have to lower it later in order to close the deal because the buyer's lender will not approve an overpriced sale.

The key to implementing these negotiation strategies is offering a superior product. The home has to show well, be in excellent working condition, and offer something that the competition does not. This will earn you to upper hand in negotiations. If buyers are not excited about the house you are selling, they will be turned off by hardball tactics and most likely walk away.

When in doubt, just ask your Top Producer. Closing is the final step in this guide and it is so important for you as a first time home seller. If you have made it this far, odds are you have experienced a long journey and have worked hard to implement the appropriate methods described in order to reach the finish line. However, you have not crossed the finish line just yet. At this point in the game, you should have an exit strategy, or a moving plan, ready to go. Your Realtor will assist you with that if needed by suggesting movers. Closing entails a lot, but your Realtor will see you through the process.

A lot of sellers make the mistake of failing to complete a full set of disclosures prior to closing. They run the risk of paying a lot of money because they did not reveal it all. Be upfront and forthcoming about any of your home's issues. Being honest will save you a lot of time and money, especially if the buyers should end up uncovering problems themselves, and they usually do. Do not forget to complete a full disclosure for your property.

Closing is when the home buyer and home seller fulfill all of the agreements made in the sales contract. A more literal translation would be that it is the transfer of money and documents so that you, the seller, can transfer ownership and possession of the property free and clear to the buyer. You will pay off all loans you still carry on the house and pay all parties who contributed documents or services to facilitate the sale and the closing.

If you agreed to make repairs to the home or any other improvements, they should be completed before the closing. The exception would be if you and the buyer had a separate contract for the improvements to be completed at a later time.

There are numerous requirements and costs associated

with closing that make it much more complex than just buying something at a store. Costs and requirements result from the sales contract, from traditional and local custom, and from local, state, and federal laws. A closing is also referred to as "settlement" because the seller, together with everyone else involved in the sale process, is "settling up" amongst all parties who provided services or documents to the transaction.

Closing usually involves the service of an escrow agent who acts as a third party that both the buyer and seller can trust and who coordinates the activities between each party according to the sale and purchase agreement. The duration of the steps required to close a real estate transaction is known as "escrow".

Right before escrow is closed, the buyer and the seller receive a closing statement from the escrow agent, who lists the purchase price and all expenses associated with buying the property and how those expenses will be allocated between the buyer and seller. At closing, the expenses that either the buyer or seller are responsible are called "closing costs", which pay for closing itself rather than for the property or any bills associated with it. Your closing costs as a seller will include various expenses, some of which are the broker's commission, the title search, any prepayment penalties accrued, and the certificate of satisfaction fee.

Do not make the mistake of overlooking any fees and expenses at closing. Home sellers throw away thousands of dollars by not requesting and confirming a list of fees beforehand. Your Realtor will review any estimated closing cost statements with you long before it is time to hand over the keys.

The main benefit to closing in escrow is that the parties and their representatives do not have to meet. They can just send the required documents to the escrow agent, who then makes sure everything is in order, then effects the settlement and the transfer. Escrow agents have the right to examine the title to make sure that there are not defects and that all conditions have been met. Once everything is in order, the escrow agent will send the seller the purchase money and record the deed for the buyer, including the mortgage if necessary.

Once all parties are satisfied and the contract is signed, a "closing date" is included. The closing date is normally a few weeks into the future to allow the buyer to get all their affairs in order. This also allows you, the seller, plenty of time to move out and finish any agreed upon projects. Once the contract closes, the buyer has the full rights to occupy the home, so you will need to make sure you are out by that time, or, if you have a problem, negotiate a working alternative recourse with the new homeowner. Some sellers are able to rent back from buyers. In some instances, depending on which part of the country you are in, the buyer only gives the seller a day or two after closing to move. In any case, before you agree to anything you have to make sure it is in writing.

You will want to prepare by having a checklist ready for your moving plan. As soon as you can, book your actual moving date. Be sure to confirm your moving date, your new address, and establish new agreements with gas, electricity, water, and telephone companies. Book a moving van, or arrange for family and friends to help you move if needed. You should have already gotten a head start on sorting all of your things and packing them away in the preparation phase before you put your home on the market, so pack up anything else you want to take with you. A great tip for packing is to make a scaled floor plan of your new place and use color coded stickers. Use a different color for each room and put the stickers on your furniture and boxes. That way those helping you move will know where everything needs to go and everything will already be in the space to which they belong.

Do not forget to set up insurance coverage for your new home, if applicable. If you are moving into a rented residence, you will have already signed a written tenancy agreement and paid a deposit. Stay alert and be aware of safety issues when moving into any new place. Check all of the doors, windows, and locks. Make sure smoke alarms are functional and you have an emergency escape plan in the event of a fire. You may have covered all of your bases, but others are not always keen on doing the same. Try to have fun and get creative by unpacking and arranging your things. Bask in your security and relax knowing you have been successful in such a huge undertaking that at first seemed so confounding. Now you know that it is possible.

Conclusion

Reaching closure and achieving maximum profit for your home is subject to many different variables, which is why it is critical that you have someone fighting in your corner. Your Realtor will be able to provide you with the best strategy in each step of the selling process, from how you choose to present your home to how you will negotiate terms and offers at the closing. The best method to achieve the best outcome is subjective to a number of factors, including what situation you are in and what conditions are at play. Use this advice to your advantage and set a guideline as you conduct your own standpoint.

This guide has taken you through all of the essentials involved in selling your home for the first time, including things to consider before you sell, ensuring the house is ready for potential buyers, and what to do to speed the sale of your home. The home selling process can be complicated and confusing, but with the aid of a top producing Realtor and the tips and techniques that have brought to light, it is possible to sell your home successfully. If you follow these professional guidelines, you will put yourself in a better position, giving yourself the optimal chances allowable in this fight. so understand that it will take hard work and determination every step of the way.

Everyone wants to turn a profit, but there are many things to consider that directly influence the outcome of your success in real estate, including how a home is presented and what kind of market a home is sitting in. The real estate market can be intimidating and unfair, but navigating through it with a Top Realtor using advanced tools to ensure your success will be the best decision you make. Not everyone can sell a home and turn a profit in a particular market setting due to certain conditions, but you can be sure that, if you follow the advice provided, you will receive the maximum price attainable for your home.

As you have been shown, marketing and selling homes successfully requires thoughtfulness, planning, and creativity. The advice, examples, and tools presented in this guide will advance your efforts and abilities as a newcomer in the real estate world. You can continue with your life with a cushion of security to fall on when times are, shall we say, less than favorable. It is a comforting thought knowing that your will is the way. You can settle down in a new house with new neighbors or travel to another land and meet people from an entirely different culture. The choice is yours to make. You can do anything you set your mind to, so you can sell your home with the right information. You now have that information.

Thank you for reading "The Smart First-Time Home Seller's Guide".

I sincerely hope that you received value from this book and gain a better understanding of how you can profit the most when selling your home.
If you enjoyed this book, please take a moment to share your thoughts and leave a review on Amazon, even if it's only a few lines; it would make all the difference and would be very much appreciated!

As a gift for reading this book, I would like to share a bonus guide with you. This guide is about "Five Common Mistakes to Avoid when Selling a Home". The information in this guide itself can help you save thousands of dollars.

I hope you will enjoy it.
Thomas.K.Lutz

Bonus: Five Common Mistakes to Avoid When Selling a Home

Don't ask for too much

A costly mistake home sellers make is when they list the home for too high a selling price. Buyers usually will not buy homes which are listed above the common market value for homes selling in that particular geographical area. The seller lists the home for 10% above the market price for a home under one million dollars is pricing the home too high. The home listed for 25% above market value is way overpriced and will not sale.

The consequences from the seller's trying sale their home for too high a price can be very detrimental. The home could sit on the market for months and potential buyers will be drawn away because they will perceive there is something wrong with the home and that is why it isn't selling. Generally buyers will not look at a home that is overpriced because it is not in their list of wants for their potential dream home; this is another disadvantage of putting a home on the market for too high a price. The house sits for 3 months, 6 months or 1 year. Eventually, the seller will have to lower the price repeatedly and in the end result the house may sell for hundreds of thousands of dollars below the price other houses are comparatively selling in the same neighborhood. Here is an example of this very costly process happening.

This particular seller, of a Spanish style home, didn't interview any real estate agents before she picked one to sell her home. She picked the first one she saw off the internet because "he looked like such a nice guy." This real estate agent was from another city and he didn't know the prices homes were selling for in the seller's particular market. He promptly listed the home for 1.3 million dollars; the home sat for 90 days and the listing expired. The seller enlisted another Real Estate agent (from another town) who put the home on the market for 1.1million dollars. Months passed and no solid offers were made on the house. Then the house was re-priced below $900,000 dollars and 1 year now passes and the house still hasn't sold. By now the seller is exhausted and calls in the final real estate agent who with the seller lists the house at $625,000 dollars and the house sells immediately for cash. The sad result was other homes in this area had sold for $835,000 dollars but unfortunately this overpriced home sat on the market for too long and the market had softened. Ultimately the seller lost $210,000 dollars in profits on the sale of their home.

Just because a seller makes pricey upgrades to their homes (granite countertops, stainless steel appliances or installing an island in their kitchen) doesn't mean a buyer is willing to pay out the extra money for these improvements when other homes in the neighborhood are selling for lower prices. The buyer will gravitate toward the lower priced home especially when the home meets all their needs and at a much lower selling price.

Another mistake home sellers make in over pricing a home is when they ignore the way Real Estate agents value the selling price of a home. Let's say the seller picks a number just because the number is a nice round figure and sounds good to the seller. They may have read of a home selling for a healthy figure in their area so they figure their home is worth X amount more than this house sold for and list it for that price. Chances are slim they will sell their overpriced home because they didn't do their homework and ask a Real Estate agent or an Appraiser to make a realistic appraisal of the value of their home. They just chose a random number they thought they could sell their home for. Real Estate agents will ignore an overpriced listing when the seller is being unreasonable in refusing to lower the price of their home. Agents will work with reasonable home sellers not unreasonable ones. The Home seller will miss out on the knowledge, expertise and experience the Real Estate agent could have brought to the selling process This is detrimental when the seller refuses to lower the price on a house listed for too high of a selling price.

Don't try and sell the house on your own unless you know what you are doing.

A top selling mistake homeowners make when selling their home is when they try and sell the home without the help of a Real Estate agent. The home seller usually doesn't have the experience of knowing what the going prices of homes are selling in their area nor do they have the experience to negotiate the best selling price for their home when the selling process reaches that stage.

Generally "For sale by owner homes" sell for $41,000 on average lower than homes sold using a Real Estate agent and the homes take 19 days longer to sell. Buyers aren't willing to pay higher prices on homes that are being sold by the owner because there is no Real Estate agent involved. Unless the seller has sold 6 or more homes or in their neighborhood homes are selling within 1 or 2 days it really is not advisable for a home seller to try and sell their home on their own.

The Real Estate agent can handle problems that come up during the selling process that they have encountered before where if the non-experienced home seller runs into these obstacles they will not have the experience to work through the problems. Another error (when they try and sell their home on their own) is they have to deal with all the potential buyers one on one and this can take a heavy toll on the home seller. The Real Estate agent also has the perception to weed out people who are not interested in buying the home but just want to "look" at it. The home seller may not pick up on these type of "buyers." Disclosure laws run plentiful these days and if the home seller isn't knowledgeable in the intricacies of these laws they can take a lot of liability on themselves. Unless the home seller knows a lawyer or a friend who can guide you through the legal process, it would be advisable to hire a Real Estate agent who is very well versed in the disclosure laws.

Selling a "house by owner" leaves the seller in a very negative circumstance because the odds are statistically stacked against the home owner. The owner may perceive they have good marketing skills and won't need a realtor. This is not true because the home owner who is inexperienced at selling his home will run into many marketing obstacles (he doesn't know how to work through) that a realtor has already experienced and knows how to navigate.

This lesson is taken from http://www.greatcoloradohomes.com/blog/top-5-mistakes-when-selling-your-home.html

This young couple decided to sell their first home with no prior experience. They felt they had satisfactory marketing skills to sale the house they didn't. They decided to owner finance the house; just to get rid of it. The process ended up costing them much more time and money than they thought. They regretted that decision for years to come.

Don't neglect to fix things that are broken

The homeowner should never be in such a big hurry to sale their house that they neglect needed repairs that are obvious. Additionally, letting any hidden repairs go will be a big mistake. The homeowner will benefit immensely to fix the repairs in their home before they put their house on the market to sale. The worst thing a home seller can do is to neglect repairs and have potential buyers walk through the house and notice the needed repairs. When this happens the buyer will be unwilling to pay a higher price for the house and he will offer a lower price. He will also ask for credit from the seller to cover the range of the potential repairs and this could cost the seller many unexpected expenses.

The entry hall is the gateway to the rest of the house and is the first area the buyers will notice where repairs have been neglected. Loose door knob, hole in the front door screen or is there a hole in the front hallway wall? These may seem like little issues but these little issues can add up to a home not selling. The buyer will be wondering what is broken behind the scenes and what type of condition the rest of the house is in. The buyer will be looking for other repairs needed throughout the rest of the house. The buyer sees that cracked window and the crack in the kitchen floor he may be thinking there is structural issues in the foundation of the house. The buyer may notice water stains on the bedroom ceiling could this be signs of a roof leak? These repair signs speak (to the buyers) that the house is full of problems and the house repeatedly loses potential buyers because of neglected repairs.

The homeowner should do a walkthrough of his home before he puts it on the market like he was walking through it the first time. He may notice the holes in the wall, the gutters leaking. Those doorknobs are loose and what about the leak under the kitchen sink? The hardwood floor around the refrigerator is rotted and warped. Better for the homeowner to find these repair needs instead of the buyer or real estate agent walking through the house.

The home sellers could find themselves in a situation where they may have to enter into Real Estate repair negotiations with the buyer. Then you get into what is reasonable and not reasonable in repair expectations on both sides. The seller thinks the repair requests are unreasonable and the buyer refuses to enter into a contract because the seller won't accept the buyers repair requests. Naturally the buyer will back out of the deal and the sale of the home is lost. The next buyer comes along and enters into a second round of Real Estate negotiations with the seller. This buyer is even more demanding in what repairs in the house he expects the seller to agree to. The seller refuses to agree to these repair expectations. Another sell lost because the seller did not fix the items in the house that needed repair before the house went on the market.

http://www.thestar.com/business/personal_finance/2013/06/09/toronto_home_sale_leads_to_repair_clause_dispute.html records a valuable lesson for home sellers to fix all parts of their home before they try and sell it. There was a couple in Canada who had built a home in 1997 and decided to sale it after living in it for seven years. The buyer agreed to buy the home for $1.995 million there were repairs that weren't made to the house before it was put up for sale. The repairs were as follows: there was a broken window, flue caps for the chimney and some minor electrical repairs. But there were major repairs that were needed to the roof. The roof was flat instead of sloped in two areas and the water was pooling in the flat areas of the roof which could lead to leaks. The buyer and seller agreed on a conditional contract that all the repairs would be fixed ahead of time before the house was sold. The house sold and three years later the buyer noticed that there was a leak in the dining room beneath the flat roof. The new owner took the original owners to court and sued them for $20,000 dollars to replace the flat roof with a sloping roof. The judge ruled against the new owner and the sellers were off the hook. But the point is that if the sellers would have fixed the flat roofs before putting the house on the market they could have saved the trouble of negotiating a Real Estate repair contract. They also would have avoided being sued and having to pay legal fees for ending up in court. They also tarnished their reputation as honest people to deal with in a home selling situation. So it's advisable to have the home inspected before putting on it the market and fixing all the problems that need attention ahead of time.

Don't get emotionally involved in the sale of your home

One of the common mistakes homeowners should avoid when selling their homes-never become emotionally attached to a house when you put it up for sale. Distance yourself by making changes within and outside the home that will attract the most buyers and bring top dollar in your sale. True you created a lot of priceless memories in that house and you put your own personality into every corner of the house. But this doesn't mean the buyer will share in your taste of customized furniture throughout the house or your choice of lemon yellow paint in the bedroom because it's a favorite color. Painting the rooms in neutral colors will go a long way in attracting buyers to your home.

Home sellers may have grown up in a house since early childhood and will have a very hard time emotionally letting go when it comes time to sale their home. There are many drawbacks to not "letting go" of a home when the time comes to sale it. The owners have put their personalized touch in the house over a long period of time and tend to have a hard time detaching from their home and looking at it as a "product". When home sellers insist on putting their homes on the Real Estate market for a higher listing than they are really worth, they are headed for trouble because they aren't ready to sell their home.

Classic signs of a homeowner being emotionally attached to his homes at selling time will surface when he isn't willing to negotiate with the buyer on the selling price of the home. The seller will not listen to any suggestions the Real Estate agent makes to improve the appearance of the house to increase the chance of selling the home for the highest dollar value. Let's say the Real Estate agent walks through the house with the seller. There are personal photos or sports memorabilia crowding the walls at every turn and the Real Estate agent suggests to remove all these items. But the seller refuses to remove these items because this is their home and they don't want let go of the customized touch they worked so hard to achieve over the years. The seller is refusing to detach themselves from their home and look at it as if the home was a product.

In1996 there a home seller in Colorado, who became too emotionally involved in the sale of his house. The home sat on the market for months with little activity from buyers and there seemed to be no interest in his home. The seller of the home chose this particular Real Estate agent because his company guaranteed if the home did not sale the company would buy it.

The seller was very emotionally involved in the sale of the home and wouldn't let the Real Estate agent do his job. Finally, the home seller was so disgusted with the lack of progress on the sale of the home, that he called the Real Estate agent and told him to take the home off the market and to have the Real Estate Company buy the home. The Real Estate agent tried to explain to the seller that the company would buy the home for below its market value and the homeowner would lose money on the sale .The   seller wouldn't listen and insisted the company buy the home so he could get it sold. The agent finally convinced the seller to leave the house on the market. The home finally sold but if the seller wouldn't have listened to the agent he could have lost thousands of dollars on the sale of his home. He was too emotionally involved in the sale of the house and it almost cost him a lot of money.

Refusing to negotiate on the sale price of the home

The final mistake home sellers make is when they refuse to negotiate the selling price of the home. The seller puts their home up for sale and they list it for the full selling price. A buyer comes along and tours the house and absolutely falls in love with the home. The buyer makes a full price offer on the house. The seller rejects the full price offer and gives the buyer no reason why the offer was refused. The seller will not even negotiate the price of the home. By refusing the full price of the house and not leaving room for negotiating on the price of the home the buyer moved on and the seller lost the sell.

Seller puts an older home on the market for sale. The buyer does a walkthrough of the house and likes the house. The buyer talked the seller down $4,000 on the price of the house. There was an inspection done and the house needed $10,000 worth of repairs. The buyer asked the seller to reduce the price of the house by $9,000 dollars so the buyer could cover the cost of the repairs. The seller refused and told the buyer they would rather take the house off the market than lower the price by $9,000 dollars. They refused to negotiate anymore with the buyer. The buyer moved on and the seller lost a sale because they wouldn't negotiate the selling price of the home any further.

This final example of a seller losing the sale of their home because they wouldn't negotiate is taken from **http://www.zillow.com/advice-thread/First-Time-Buyer-Seller-Refuses-to-Negotiate-on-Price/391883/** this first time home buyer found a home they really liked. The selling price was listed at $119,000 dollars and the buyer made a healthy offer of $110,000 dollars. The seller rejected the offer and came back with a counter offer of $119,000 dollars. The house was purchased for $110,000 dollars in 2009 and had been depreciating ever since. Upon the inspection other issues were detected but the owners still refused to come down from their $119,000 dollar price. They lost the sale of the home because they wouldn't negotiate with the buyer on the selling price of their home.

Avoid these five home selling mistakes and you will have much better success in selling your home. Good Luck!

Made in the USA
Lexington, KY
11 May 2018